Successful
Empowerment
in a week

Steve Morris and
Graham Willcocks

Headway · Hodder & Stoughton

British Library Cataloguing in Publication Data
A catalogue record for this title is available from the British Library

ISBN 0 340 64330 7
First published 1995
Impression number 10 9 8 7 6 5 4 3 2 1
Year   1999 1998 1997 1996 1995

Typeset by Multiplex Techniques Ltd, Orpington, Kent.
Printed in Great Britain for Hodder & Stoughton Educational,
a division of Hodder Headline Plc, 338 Euston Road, London
NW1 3BH by St Edmundsbury Press, Bury St Edmunds,
Suffolk.

the Institute
of Management

F O U N D A T I O N

The Institute of Management (IM) is at the forefront of management development and best management practice. The Institute embraces all levels of management from students to chief executives. It provides a unique portfolio of services for all managers, enabling them to develop skills and achieve management excellence.

For information on the benefits of membership, please write to:

Department HS
Institute of Management
Cottingham Road
Corby
Northants NN17 1TT
Tel. 01536 204222
Fax 01536 201651

This series is commissioned by the Institute of Management Foundation.

C O N T E N T S

■ I N T R O D U C T I O N ■

Empowerment is a current management buzzword that means something both complex and difficult. However, it doesn't have to be, and in the coming week you will see that you can empower people, if you are prepared to take some simple and positive steps.

The chances are that you, like most managers and supervisors, have experienced an authoritarian approach to management from your managers as you worked your way up. This experience can form the impression that, because that is how your manager did it, it is the only way to manage. However, it isn't, and it isn't usually the best way, either. Putting the emphasis on control, and issuing orders and instructions works in some situations, but it can smother the human potential of the people working for you. Your staff have brains and they want to do well, so what is stopping you from releasing all that potential and getting it working for you?

The short answer is: you. Having to let go and thus empower people might sound as if you are going to lose your grip, but it doesn't work that way. Trust people and they almost invariably perform well for themselves, for you and for the organisation.

This week, we will follow the plan below:

Sunday	Preparing strong foundations
Monday	Barriers to empowerment
Tuesday	Identifying hidden talents
Wednesday	Keeping control
Thursday	The 'easy-win' day
Friday	The importance of good communication
Saturday	Review

Preparing strong foundations

Empowerment will not happen on its own. It is something you will need to lead your people through. Because of this you need to do plenty of preparation.

It's important before you get started to examine your own attitudes to empowerment and to be clear about just what you want to achieve. The reason for this is that much of empowerment is in the mind. To empower people you need to look at your own, and their, attitudes. You may have to ask yourself some fundamental questions too about why people come to work. If you believe that people are basically unambitious then empowerment may not be for you. If you believe that people are always capable of more than they do at present then read on and enjoy. Empowerment is about valuing people and understanding the contribution they can make. So before you actually start an empowerment programme it's important to get these issues and your own attitudes towards empowerment very clear.

- Step 1: Be clear what empowerment means to you
- Step 2: Be clear about the issues
- Step 3: More personal preparation
- Step 4: Look for help
- Step 5: Be clear about your starting point

Step 1: Be clear what empowerment means to you

Like a lot of new ideas, people can get trapped in the jargon and never be really clear what it all means. If you are going to either introduce or implement empowerment you need to be absolutely clear in your own mind what it is, what it will mean for you and what you want to achieve with it.

The way you define empowerment depends on a number of factors. If you are following a company policy or empowerment initiative then it is likely that many of the parameters will be sketched out. You may inherit a definition. If you are starting from scratch then you are free to develop your own definition. However, whatever boat you are in, it is important to get a working definition clear in your mind.

A definition of empowerment
So, what we need is a definition first. Get a big sheet of paper and write down as many definitions of empowerment as you can and then choose your favourite. Alternatively you could draw up a short checklist of some of the effects of empowerment and work from that.

What is empowerment:? A checklist approach
1 It is a way of allowing front-line staff to delight the customer
2 It is about letting my people get on with the job without undue interference from me
3 It is about my people taking responsibility for the experience customers get
4 It is about letting those people closest to the customer have the power to sort any problems out
5 It's about getting rid of the daft bureaucracy that stops people doing their job
6 It is a way of helping front-line staff to put their ideas for improvements at work into practice

Whatever definition you come up with, remember that empowerment isn't something you should do just for its own sake. The whole focus of empowerment is that it should improve the service you offer to your customers through the increased performance of your team – both individually and as a whole.

It is important here to be clear that empowerment is not the same as delegation. Delegation means that you decide what people should take on. Empowerment means they take responsibility for decisions and their work. Empowerment is not telling people to buy the tea bags from the local corner shop.

What do you want to achieve?
So now we have a definition, but what do you want to achieve from empowerment? It is no good just airily saying you want to empower people with no real reason for doing

it. Be clear about what you actually want to achieve and this will help you guide the whole process.

And why is it important to be clear what you want from empowerment? Well it:

- Takes time
- Takes effort
- Will mean you have to examine your role as a manager

It can also be:

- Rewarding
- Fun
- An excellent way of getting the best from your people

On another sheet of paper, write down five things you want to achieve through empowerment. You can use this as a kind of checklist throughout the week and in the weeks beyond. Try to be realistic about what is likely to happen. You also need to be positive too.

What you want to achieve: a checklist
1 What do you want to achieve for yourself? What are your personal goals?
2 What do you want your team to achieve? Empowerment is a team effort so start thinking about what you want your team to get out of it
3 What do you want your organisation to achieve?
4 What differences do you want customers to notice?

Now, write down your main priorities from the list you have generated. What are the main three of four things you want to achieve this week.

Step 2: Be clear about the issues

The next step is to make a list of some of the big issues that empowerment is likely to highlight so that you will be prepared for them. This is important because empowerment is dynamic and does lead to change. Here is a start.

Information
Empowerment enables teams to exchange information freely. Information is important because any successful empowerment initiative is based on improved communications. You will find that people will want to swap ideas and suggestions about the way they work and ideas for improving the service. They will also need to be reassured that they are actually doing the 'right thing'.

Resources
You may well need to put some resources in place to help people become empowered – so you need to start thinking early on about what you have at your disposal and whether you will need to start lobbying your boss to get some money for part of your plan. Some of the resources you might need to find are:

Money, of course. Possibly a small or not so small fighting fund. Your empowered team may come up with an improvement suggestion that requires a small budget from you, or indeed for them to hold a small budget over a period of time. In this case if you have to ask them to hang on for a few weeks for you to get approval, it will get your empowerment push off to a rather unconvincing start.

Training opportunities. Your team may need something like assertiveness training to help them take more responsibility. This will need to be paid for and cover provided.

New *fixtures and fittings*. You can't expect your team to start feeling empowered if they work in an uncondusive work environment.

Roles
You need to be clear about your role at the moment and how you think it might change if you empower your team. There is no point announcing that you are going to start empowerment if you change your mind after a couple of days or indeed if you simply carry on working in the same old way as before.

Your people
They have a lot to offer, so empowerment means, almost

like Sherlock Holmes, that you need to be finding out what they can offer and what they enjoy, what they are good at and then helping to match up their talents with the objectives you set.

Flexibility
You may need to adopt a different approach. Empowerment works when the old hierarchies and routines are broken down, and so you will need to be flexible yourself.

Step 3: More personal preparation

Now that you have started to look at some of the ideas about some of the issues that might be at stake, it's important to start clearly examining your own motives and hopes and fears. Go through the following checklist and answer the questions honestly.

- I'm interested in empowerment because it's a new fad
- I'm interested in empowerment but I don't really want to give up any of the jobs I enjoy or the authority I hold
- Empowerment is easy; you just tell people to go away and get on with it
- I don't need to empower my team. I'm the boss, and they should just listen to what I have to tell them
- Empowerment is dangerous. It's likely to end up in a free-for-all
- I'm only doing it to keep in with the boss

If you answered 'yes' to any of these questions, the chances
are that you are going to find it hard to be successful with
your empowerment because you haven't examined your
attitudes clearly enough. If you start out with this rather
negative frame of mind then it is unlikely you will get very
far. Instead, address some of your fears and try to think
your way round them.

Be clear in your mind before you start that empowerment
does not need to be a free-for-all. It can and must be
controlled.

The second issue you need to be clear about is your own
attitude towards your own power. Empowerment may
mean giving up some of the things you like and exchanging
your present job for a slightly different one. You need to be
comfortable with the implications of this. The empowered
manager may no longer be a kind of benign dictator. You
may need to swap this role and instead become more of an
empowerer/facilitator, helping your staff to achieve. This
means a number of things.

- You may need to swap the buzz factor of being needed
  for your great wisdom. Many managers like feeling
  needed and being the fount of all knowledge in the
  workplace. With empowerment you are likely to cast
  off your oracle role for a more facilitative role which
  aims at people doing things for themselves and
  thinking for themselves.
- You may need to hand over the keys to the stationery
  cupboard metaphorically speaking. If you are going to
  give people a chance to take responsibility you need to
  give them the authority to take it.

Your hopes and fears

To round off this step, draw up a list of your hopes and fears for empowerment. Be honest. Don't skirt around your fears or bury your head in the sand and hope they go away. Get them all out in the open. You need to be prepared and to start drawing up plans. What's more, it is important to start coming up with answers to your fears, because if one thing is certain, it is that your people and maybe your boss will share some of them. You might find the following list helpful.

I fear that empowerment may:
- Do me out of a job
- Lead to people seeing me as weak
- Let people take advantage of me
- Be chaotic

I hope that empowerment will:
- Let me get the best out of my people
- Increase customer satisfaction
- Change the way we work around here
- Let people bring their brains to work with them

Step 4: Look for help

Now you have looked a bit closer at your attitudes to empowerment, and what it means, you need to start thinking early on about what help you will need to make empowerment work for you. We have already seen that empowerment is not something you can just turn on, like water from a tap. It's something you need to plan, and it's something about which you may come into conflict with other people. After all, empowering people may threaten some. Ask the following question: 'Who will be able to help me in the coming week?'

Identifying your champions
Try to come up with a list of people who will champion the cause. It might include your boss or your boss's boss. It might include other people in your team. It might even include friends and colleagues you ran ring up, talk to and bounce ideas off. Who are the main people in your department you think will approve and help you make the idea of empowerment a reality? Indeed you may already have had people coming and talking to you and asking for their jobs to be enhanced, or for you to delegate things to them.

- Come up with a list of three of four people who you think will actually champion your ideas and help your empowerment work over the next week

This activity may look straightforward but there are a number of pitfalls and there is some advice to offer.

1 You need to identify people who you think will be positive and open to new ideas.
2 You need people who will help win over their colleagues. Try to identify one of your team whom the others hold in high esteem. If you can get him or her on your side, you will have a greater chance of success.
3 You want level headed people too; you don't want someone who will quickly get swept along and then, equally quickly, become frustrated and disillusioned.
4 Don't make too many assumptions about people. All too often the people who seem a little bolshy or difficult may be the ones who really make it work. So, if you are working with people outside your team, don't get taken in by the corporate mythology. The 'bad lot' may simply be a person with a brain and bags of talent waiting to help you make empowerment happen.

Identify enemies

Now ask yourself, who do you think might be very negative towards the idea of empowerment? Don't just think about the people in your team, but any bosses or anyone else in the organisation who you think might put a damper on things. You need to be aware of where any blockages might occur so you can tackle them fully.

You may be able to get a feel for those who:

- Will be negative but are unlikely to put paid to any plans you have
- Have real power to damage the initiative

When you have done this you will start getting a clear idea of the people you need to speak to tomorrow. You will also get a feeling for some of those you might need to win over, or those who seem very difficult to win over and who may need to be bypassed.

Step 5: Be clear about your starting point

A key thing is to get a clear idea in your mind of where your organisation or team are at the moment. It's very difficult to start empowering people unless you know where you are coming from.

There are different ways of looking at organisations, but the key phrase here is 'organisational culture'. Put simply, an organisational culture means 'the way we do things around here'. If your organisation is very hierarchical and resistant to change, you are likely to have a much tougher job of empowering than if your organisation is already open, communicates freely, and allows people to express themselves and fulfil their potential.

Look at the following four different kinds of culture, and decide whereabouts your organisation is. The further towards the bottom of the list, the less resistance you are likely to face. If you are working in an organisation towards the top of this list, you may need to adjust your aims or expect things to take slightly longer.

Power culture
This is probably the most traditional of cultures found in organisations. In the power culture, there tends to be one

central power source, usually the person who actually set up the business. This means that the ideas behind the business tend to come from this one person, who is very dominant. The power comes very much from the centre of this organisation, spreading out rather like a web. In this sort of organisation it's very difficult to have any sort of power unless you are near the centre of that web.

This has implications for empowerment. If the idea for empowerment comes out of the blue or from someone not in the power centre, then it is likely to be greeted with horror and seen as a threat by those in power. Even if it comes from the centre, old habits die hard and it may be a struggle to get the power holders to let go and make taking responsibility a reality.

Role culture
Organisations with a role culture work with power concentrated at the top and with very set ways of doing things. They have a power pyramid. In the role culture the job description is king and people can be penalised for showing initiative or trying new things. These organisations are stable, but very resistant to change. They are the kind of organisation where people may have a job description and stick to it, and where innovation and new ideas are seen as positive disadvantages, threatening the status quo. A typical example of a role culture organisation is the civil service.

Typically the role culture organisation has levels and levels of management. People tend to move up the organisation incrementally and at a snail's pace and possibly as a result of time serving. Privileges, rank and daft routines are cherished and defended. People doing more than their jobs are seen as a threat and as dangerous mavericks. Role culture organisations are often referred to as traditional. This is not fertile soil for empowerment.

Task culture
These are often small and new organisations which work very much on a project team basis. Architects and designers often have organisations with task cultures.

Person culture
This is where there are few structures, and when they do exist they are just to support individuals rather than control them. They tend to be open and are tolerant of staff's learning. They may invest heavily in training and are often receptive to new ideas. They essentially trust the people who work there and are probably looking to give them learning opportunities. This is good fertile ground for empowerment.

Activity
The last thing you should do today is decide just which
one of these cultures matches your place of work. You
may find there is no exact match with the four cultures
outlined above, but they will give you a good starting
point. Think about your experiences in the past. How
tolerant of mistakes is the place you work? Are people
given a chance to take on extra responsibility if they
ask for it? If you come up with a new idea would the
response be 'Do it' or 'That will have to go to
committee' or 'leave the thinking to us; you get on with
the job'?

Summary

To recap, you have spent today examining your own
attitudes and:

- Deciding what you want from empowerment
- Deciding what empowerment means to you
- Identifying some of the people who can help your
  empowerment during the week, and some of the
  blockages you might face
- Getting a clear idea of where you are starting from,
  and how much work you are likely to need to do to
  make empowerment work for you

Above all, you need to realise that empowerment needs to
be planned, and that you have a big role in leading it. This
section may also have helped put to rest some of your own
anxieties about what empowerment might mean.

Barriers to empowerment

It is now your first day in work with empowerment on top of the agenda. You probably feel raring to go, but it's important not to rush in too quickly and put your people off. You still need to do more preparation. It is unlikely you will be able to change everything at once, so it is best to go softly softly and win people over more gradually. Empowerment can seem like a big threat to some people, so it is important to take things a step at a time. Today we will look at:

- Bringing down the barriers
- A barriers checklist

Knocking on doors
The following gives the flavour of the approach we favour.

Imagine you are standing in a long corridor surrounded by closed doors. You want to get into a room. It doesn't matter which one, you just want to get out of the corridor. You have a number of options. One of them is to plant explosives and blow down the door. It could work but there is likely to be a lot of mess and you might end up getting hurt. Better by far to try the handles first. Some of the doors may already be open.

So it is with empowerment. If you get your preparation and research right some of the doors that look firmly closed and seem to be real barriers may in fact be opened easily.

Bringing down the barriers

Because empowerment is about allowing people to take responsibility, you need to think very carefully about the barriers that are in their way. In fact, write the following questions in big letters, pin them to your wall and try to answer them afresh every day.

What is stopping my team from taking responsibility at the moment?

How can we use empowerment to offer our customers a better service?

If the first answer you came up with to the first of the two questions is 'me', then you know you have some work to do on your own attitudes and behaviour.

However, these aren't the only questions to ask yourself; indeed we'll come to a few more later today.

Looking for clues
It is important not to be too one-dimensional in your

approach. Barriers to empowerment can take many shapes or forms, some of which are quite unexpected. If you want to make empowerment a success you need to cover every angle and come up with a plan for dismantling all the barriers and not just the obvious ones.

Step 1: Do a personal brainstorm
Put yourself in the place of your people or look at the barriers you yourself face. The key is to make sure you leave no stone unturned. Sometimes the best motivated empowerment programmes can fall by the wayside because managers and people taking part have ignored one crucial piece of information and one crucial barrier that stops people performing. Draw up a list of all the barriers you face to empowerment yourself and a list of all the barriers you *think* your staff face (you will test the list in reality a little later today, so be prepared for some surprises).

You may want to ask the following fundamental questions (you can ask your team the same questions a little later).

- What do I think are the barriers that are stopping my staff becoming empowered?
- How many of these can I do something about now?
- How many can I do something about in the near future?
- How many can I do something about in the long term?

Step 2: Get your team together and test it out
It is time to involve your team in this process and start finding out things from them. In fact, a simple rule for anything to do with empowerment is 'involve your people'.

So get your people together. Give yourself about an hour to do this exercise. You don't want to feel hurried and people like to be given a chance to air their views.

Your task is to try to get your people to tell you all the barriers they think they face. Explain first, why you are holding the meeting and what you want to get out of it. Be very clear about what you mean by barriers. Try to make it fun and enjoyable. This will help people to discuss openly the things they feel are stopping them taking responsibility at the moment.

If you have access to one, get hold of a flipchart. You can then act as scribe. Write down all the barriers people come up with. Don't knock back people's ideas or try to argue against the barriers they come up with. It is not your job to persuade them out of feeling there are barriers. Don't be frightened by the odd silence or panicked into doing all the talking yourself, although you may need to move the meeting on a little from time to time. Above all try not to look too hurt in case you put people off!

The chances are you will end up with a number of flipchart pages filled with kind of things that stopped people performing in the past, or that they are anxious might stop them performing well in the future.

Be calm; it might seem at first that there are so many barriers that the whole empowerment process is untenable. Instead, show that you are willing to listen and get every possible barrier out into the open.

When you have got them all written down, start sorting them under headings.

If it is difficult to hold this meeting in the office try to find a way of getting your people together outside work. You might be able to pop out to lunch and have a less formal discussion about barriers. Whatever way you do it, do try to get people to *tell* you about the barriers they face. Don't just make up your mind about the barriers you *think* they face without asking them. The chances are you will be wrong or overlook simple but damaging blocks to empowerment.

Step 3: Draw up a barriers hit list
When you have got a sense of the order of these different barriers the next thing is to start tackling them. Get another sheet of flipchart paper and write down all the barriers you can tackle straight away. Make a hit list of those barriers you want to tackle within this first week. Then make another list of the barriers you can tackle in the medium and longer terms. It's important, though, to think also about how you can measure whether you have tackled the barriers successfully. You may also come up with a list of cost-free ways you can overcome barriers.

In a hospital one of the barriers cleaning staff came up with was their ancient and starchy uniforms. They pointed out that patients didn't take them seriously as a result and this put the blocks on any empowerment process. An SOS call around the hospital managed to locate some newer uniforms hidden away in a store that had never been used. Within the hour the cleaners had new uniforms, the hospital had brought this about cost-free and the empowerment exercise was up and running.

Step 4: Come up with a way of monitoring success

You have developed your hit list but how will you know if those barriers have come down for good? For each idea you come up with, try to come up with two or three ways of measuring whether you have been successful. One company identified a major barrier as the way managers always said 'yes, but' to any idea from front-liners. In the past, this tendency put a stop to most new ideas. They set themselves the target of replacing 'yes, but' with 'yes' and their way of monitoring it was to count every 'yes, but' uttered in the department. Only when there were more 'yes' answers than 'yes, buts' would they know the barriers had come down.

A barriers checklist

The following are some of those barriers we have identified and you may come across too. Look through them and see how many you have on your list.

It's important not to just look at the obvious barriers to empowerment people face. Try to be broad and wide, and look for some of the intangible things that stop your people performing.

Barrier 1: Structure

How is your department and organisation structured? You might find when you look at the reporting links that there are many layers of management. If you have a very bureaucratic structure like this then it's much more difficult for people on the front line to take responsibility. It's unlikely that you will be able to change the structure of your organisation overnight but you may be able to do something in your own department. For instance:

- You may be able to start working in a more informal team-oriented way
- You may also be able to lobby some of your managers to help change things

Ready steady Freddie

A manager at a health centre wanted to work in a more empowered team oriented way. However, like much of the health service her health centre was rigidly structured and there seemed little scope for front-liners to show initiative and start taking responsibilities. The manager knew that everyone was concerned with the state of the centre and the poor fixtures and fittings. She persuaded her boss to allow her to set up a health centre improvement group to look for ways forward. She asked the centre's caretaker, Freddie, if he would like to sit on the committee along with the centre's GPs and health professionals. He said that he would. Within weeks Freddie was driving the team, coming up with ideas and designing plans for a new lobby area. He was a great success.

The manager's success was that she managed to start altering the highly unempowering structure at the health centre through this team approach. Had she suggested changing the structure cold, nothing would have happened.

Barrier 2: Those old routines

Ask yourself, what routines have built up in your department over the years and how these act as barriers to empowerment. You may indeed find that there are significant barriers here. Have fun with these routines. Why not set a task for your team to come up with the daftest barrier they face and give a prize for it.

For instance, in one home economics department in a school, a routine had built up that the keys to the saucepan cupboard were always left with the department head. This meant that any time a teacher wanted to get equipment out he or she had to go to the department head to get hold of the keys. For a start this was demeaning to some teachers who had been at the school for over 20 years, but more to the point, in the terms of empowerment this senseless routine in fact stopped people taking responsibility.

The watchword here, as is often with empowerment, is trust. The routine simply backed up the fact that the people in charge did not trust their subordinates, their staff, to do a good job.

Routines can be barriers when they:
- Cause staff unnecessary hassle
- Make people feel they have to grovel to get something
- Make people feel they are not fit to be trusted (it is amazing how people act in the way you expect them to act!)
- Cause inconvenience to everyone – especially customers

Try to come up with a list of senseless and bureaucratic routines that you could scrap at once. Make sure you take your staff along with you on this because they may resist it otherwise. Ask them what routines they find most unhelpful and then try to do something about them. But beware, some people feel comfortable with their routines and so they may need to be gently persuaded out of them.

Barrier 3: Psychological
This is an important one, and the one that people often ignore. Sometimes empowerment is blocked because of the attitudes of those taking part. Look for psychological barriers in a number of different places.

- You might find that despite all the good words and intentions some people higher up the organisation actually aren't very keen on empowerment – especially if they think it will cost them more time or money.
- You might find that some of your own team are hostile to the idea and feel that they want to hang on to their own power. In short you may find that your team do not want to empower their junior staff because they

feel it might either do them out of a job or sweep away the things they have worked hard for. Acknowledge these concerns but be firm about the direction you want to go in.

- You might find, more understandably, that your team are anxious, and their anxiety or fear of failure is actually holding back the empowerment process. One of the keys to empowerment is that people take responsibility. You may find that there is a psychological barrier to this to start with. It is something you will have to work on, and break down, by showing people that it's OK to be empowered, and if they make mistakes you won't come down on them like a ton of bricks. Above all you need to show them that you will be there to help them through.

- You may find that your team are anxious and reluctant to go along with you because they fear change. It is important to recognise this as a legitimate concern.

- You may find when you are looking at the psychological barriers that you have something of the 'old lag' syndrome. This means that some long-established staff might be very reluctant to do things in a new way, and may actively resist the empowerment drive. You may find a degree of cynicism and a desire to protect privileges. You need to be clear about who these people are, and see what you can do about their attitudes.

The most important thing with these psychological barriers is to work hard to get them all into the open. When people express their reservations, you can work on them and help them to overcome them. If people do not express their reservations they can fester and work against the empowerment process.

A SWOT analysis   People do sometimes feel uncomfortable discussing the barriers they face. One structured way of identifying the psychological barriers is to do a SWOT analysis with your team. This allows people to talk about themselves within a safe and structured process.

Find a room you can meet in. The maximum number you should involve is around eight people. You will need a flipchart and plenty of drawing pins or blue tac. Explain to staff that you want everyone to feel free to play a part in the discussion. Then write up the following four words:

- Strengths
- Weaknesses
- Opportunities
- Threats

You then ask your team to work through these headings with you in relation to the empowerment process. When they call out responses write them on the flipchart. After half an hour or so you should have generated lots of ideas. Take a short break, have a joke and then come back and summarise your findings with the team. Pick out the main findings under each heading and thank people for their help.

SWOT acts as a non-threatening way of allowing people to express their reservations about empowerment and the psychological barriers they can see ahead of them.

Barrier 4: Physical
You are likely to find some very real physical barriers. Take the following example.

The coach station
If you visited one particular coach station two years ago it was an empowerment nightmare. The ticket office was two floors up and the customer restaurant about 400 metres away. The ticket hall had no chairs and no recognised queuing mechanism. People frequently queued for an hour only to be told they had queued in the wrong place and would need to start again. There was no phone in the ticket hall and no information boards for customers about any delays. With the best will in the world, staff could not have been empowered if they wanted to be. The actual physical barriers were such that if a staff member felt it was right to offer a refund to a customer or a cup of tea or some helpful advice they couldn't. By the time the customer got to the front of the queue they were so irate, staff did not want to take responsibility for them.

Often the workplace is set out in a very unhelpful way for empowerment. You need to make sure that your department is actually set up so that front-line people can do the job they are capable of.

For instance, in a large hotel chain, an empowerment initiative stressed that staff would take responsibility for their customers and make sure that their experience of being in the hotel was always a good one. However, the hotel was set out in a very traditional way, with an imposing counter at the front, and many small and dingy rooms leading off it. Because of the layout, it was very difficult for staff to take responsibility for their customers from the very moment they entered the hotel. These customers had to pass through a kind of obstacle course before they got to the restaurant, by which point they had already 'lost' the front-liners. You may need to look at how your place of work is set out so that people can really perform.

A checklist

1 Draw a map of your workplace. How does the customer flow work? Could you improve it?
2 Where are the pressure points and bottlenecks that customers experience?
3 What are the physical things you just have to do at once?

Barrier 5: Resources

This is linked to the barrier above. One of the major barriers to empowerment may simply be that you have put no resources into it. Many people have found that allowing staff small budgets that they can use when innovating new ideas or, for instance, to give customers refunds, have been shown as major ways to drive an empowerment process. You need to look at what resources you need to make empowerment work.

No place like home

A housing organisation as part of its work, provided shared housing for young people who had been sleeping rough. The youngsters often needed counselling and help with life skills. One of the barriers faced by housing staff was that there was nowhere suitable to talk to their young tenants. If they visited them at home, they only had the bedroom, which was too personal and intrusive. If they asked the youngster to come to the office, it was too intimidating. One housing officer came up with an idea. He asked for a budget to be able to take his clients to the local cafe to discuss things over a cup of tea. In this neutral atmosphere he found the tenants felt at home and were more open about their problems. He was given the budget.

Barrier 6: Credibility

People simply may not believe you are serious about empowerment. They may feel they have heard it all before and that you really have no intention of allowing them to get on with their job and perform. If this one does come, you will need to demonstrate early on, probably in your 'easy-win' day later in the week, that you are really serious about what's happening.

One of the common barriers that people feel is that although you speak the language of empowerment, you in fact act in a quite different way personally. All too often, managers claim to have empowered front-liners, but then go charging in like the cavalry at the first sign of a problem. One hotel supervisor told us about the time he was told by his manager to 'be empowered'. One hour later, the restaurant was very busy and his manager appeared, barged him out of the way and said 'I'd better take over here, go and clear a few tables'.

If there has been a history of this happening in the past, people won't believe you when you say you are actually interested in empowerment and want them to go away and take responsibility. The message is simple. If you are a control freak and can't bring yourself to trust your team then empowerment will not work, whatever soothing words you use to the contrary.

> *A quick litmus test . . . Are you a control freak?*
> Do you:
> 1 Feel suspicious that people may be plotting behind your back if you don't keep a firm grip on things?
> 2 Find it hard to believe you do anything wrong?
> 3 Insist on seeing every piece of work your team do?

If you answered 'yes' to all three, go see a doctor.

Summary

Today you have undertaken the important job of finding what might be in your way as you work towards empowerment. In particular you:

- Identified all the important barriers you face
- Involved your staff in the process so they feel a personal investment in empowerment
- Planned ways to overcome some, or all, of the barriers
- Developed some ways of measuring whether the barriers have really come down for good

Identifying hidden talents

You have now got a real feel for some of the barriers that are in the way of empowerment. You have also started the process of developing some strategies and tactics to overcome these barriers.

Today is the day when you start tapping into some of the hidden talents within your team. This is an important day because empowerment is all about concentrating positively on your team and then allowing:

- Them to make the most of the skills and life experiences they have already built up
- You and your organisation to use those talents more regularly and more effectively

The aim of this is to help your team be more productive and offer an even better service to customers. The idea is that they will do this because they are more switched on and motivated and because staff on the front line are really the ones in the best position to improve the service on offer. On the one hand, they are the ones who your customers are likely to come into contact with. On the other hand, they are likely to have much more to offer than they already do. Today, we will look at:

- The talent rota
- Drawing up a talent rota
- Winning support
- Using the information

The empowering manager keenly believes in the ability of his team to do more than they do at present and take on more responsibility than they have at the moment. One of the touchstones of empowerment is that it is a way of freeing up the talents of your people.

You need to be very positive about the attributes and strengths resident in your people, but also dogged in your determination to help them make the most of themselves, and bring out talents that they may well not have used at work for many months or years.

Much of this is about helping people to have confidence in their own abilities and then to allow them to bring in to the workplace the kind of skills they may only use at home.

One of the key ideas behind empowerment is that people almost unerringly have much more to offer at work than they do at present. As such empowerment takes a very positive view of human nature.

The talent rota

In a recent piece of consultancy work, we worked with a large hotel chain. The manager at one of the hotels decided to put into practice empowerment because he had read about it and thought it sounded like a particularly good idea.

His first step was to draw up a talent rota. The manager did this in response to a particular problem. He had been charged by his bosses to improve the general quality of the posters and board displays around the hotel and bar area. He tried to do this himself, but found that he had no real aptitude for, or indeed particular interest in, art. The noticeboards and displays ended up looking messy. He felt embarrassed.

He put out an SOS to his staff. He told them he was looking for volunteers to come along and help him spruce the place up and make the posters look better. He was amazed by the response. He found that amongst the cleaning staff alone he had a qualified graphic designer, someone who had done Art at 'A' level, and others who did painting as a hobby. He handed over the design of the posters to a small group of people who he himself supported and managed. Given the chance to go away and shine, these people came up with posters that won the in-house award for the best design. He continued with this talent rota approach for other specific problems he came across.

Before he started this exercise he was armed only with the vaguest notion that there was untapped talent out there. This exercise confirmed this in capital letters. He actually had a wealth of talent at his disposal.

It's now time for you to draw up your own talent rota and see if you can achieve some of the success that the manager above did.

More about your attitude
However, before you even start this exercise, it's important to spend a few minutes examining your attitude again.

Keep the following thought in your head as you go about today. Outside work your people have done an amazing amount of things, and shouldered extraordinary amounts of responsibility in their lives. They may have:

- Brought up families
- Run scout groups

- Organised soccer leagues for children or adults
- Played a prominent part in the local church
- Done fund-raising for charity
- Learned to speak foreign languages
- Learned how to be counsellors
- Done Open University degrees
- Run their own business
- Bred pedigree dogs
- Done computing courses

These are just some of the hidden talents you may well discover when you start to delve a little deeper. It's very important not to feel threatened by this. The art of empowerment is to realise that other people can sometimes actually do things better than we can, and then to be able to give them the permission and support to go away and do so.

If you find out that you have a super-talented bunch who have got second languages, degrees and other attributes, you should celebrate that you can tap into all this talent. Imagine what you can achieve with all that talent at your disposal.

Drawing up a talent rota

As we have stressed elsewhere, it's important to be broad and wide in your perceptions, and in your approach to drawing up your talent rota. Remember the idea is that you are trying to get to all those hidden talents. By their very nature, hidden things may well need to be teased out into the open. It's no good just standing up and saying 'tell me about your talents'. If you do so you will probably get a lot of quizzical looks, some effrontery, and people will just clam up. You need to work at this is in a more subtle and sensitive way.

The following are just five approaches to finding out about the talent of your staff.

Three things they all share is that you will need to learn how to:

• **Ask**   It is a simple idea but one not used enough. People may be too shy to tell you about themselves. You might decide to chance asking people directly about their currently underused talents and experiences. Or, you might instigate a more organisational approach.

  A local council, for instance, has introduced a questionnaire as part of their induction process to ask people about what they do in their spare time, and some of the talents and skills they can bring from their previous jobs and life experiences. It isn't compulsory to answer these questions, but the council have found that most people do because the reason behind it is carefully explained.

• **Listen**   You need to watch out for clues and hints because people may not speak directly about themselves. One manager told us that she picked up that one of her staff was an incredibly free thinker and always challenged received wisdom. Rather than writing this off as an annoying habit she listened and saw this as a valuable attribute for the team. She used this staff member's ability to look at problems afresh when weighing up projects. Another member of staff talked about her social life. She revealed an incredibly ordered mind with social events lined up and organised months in advance. This ordered approach, again, was a worthwhile talent. The manager put both these two contrasting people together and used them as a checking mechanism every time a new project loomed. The one broadened the brush strokes, the other narrowed the risks. It was teamwork through empowerment.

- **Watch** At a recent leadership skills workshop a team were set a task involving playing cards and Lego bricks. Before the task the facilitator had appointed a leader. While he was describing the task another member of the group picked up the cards and shuffled them with ease. However, the assigned leader did not notice this and insisted on doing the shuffling himself during the exercise. This cost a lot of time and led to the group failing the exercise. The appointed leader did not watch carefully enough.

You can't do this talent rota exercise if you love the sound of your own voice. Remember you are aiming to start getting a better insight into all the areas your staff could develop and the skills they could bring to your team. You are not aiming to impress them with *your* vast interests, skills, hobbies or insight.

We now look at some useful methods you might use.

Method 1: The informal chat
This is probably still the best way of finding out about people and the most obvious. Find some time in the day, or after work, to sit down and listen to people. Make it clear with your body language that you are actually taking an interest in them and want to chat.

Avoid the following:

- Sitting with your arms folded and looking distractedly around the room
- Running an interrogation with aggressive questions and bright lights
- Jumping in and talking about yourself
- Falling asleep

Don't try to quiz your people. Instead all you are looking for is a quiet chat about the kind of things that interest them and that you may not already know about. Areas you might want to find out about are:

- What are their interests outside work?
- What hidden skills and talents do they have?
- What do they do in their spare time?
- What are their hobbies?
- What qualifications do they have, and what courses have they done?

Remember you are looking to listen actively to people. If you think about it, people give you an extraordinary range of information about themselves every day if only you listen carefully enough.

The most important thing is: what are they interested in? One of the great things about empowerment is that you can give people a chance to work in areas they are interested in, but have never previously had the chance to explore.

An organisation was about to celebrate its 50th anniversary and was planning to have a local event. During an informal chat with her secretary the manager found that she had once worked for a PR company and was bubbling with ideas about how the event could be a success. What's more she was very keen to play a part. The manager seconded her on to the event organisation committee and she played a major part in the success of the event. She wrote the press releases, acted as MC, organised the team of helpers, coordinated the stalls and made sure people stuck around to clear up the mess.

Method 2: One-to-ones
You may actually have at work, sessions where you sit
down and have one-to-one discussions with your people
about the way their jobs are going. You might find some
time here to drop in a question about areas they feel they are
currently underused in. The chances are, if you ask this
question, that your people will try and think of things they
usually do at work. The art, as far as you are concerned, is to
make it clear that you don't just want to know about the
areas they are involved in at work, but some of the areas
they are involved in outside of work, that they feel they
might be able to bring to you.

Method 3: The grapevine
You can rely on information coming through from
supervisors. Supervisors are often a mine of interesting
information about people and their interests. You may well
be able to find out something these people are interested in.
But always ask positive questions. You aren't looking to
pick up a load of tittle-tattle.

However, make sure you don't simply write people off
because of what you *hear* about them. You may hear that
someone is lazy and uncommitted, but people may behave
in a lethargic way if they feel undervalued or experience has
taught them that it simply doesn't do to try.

Listen to the following tale:

When I started I was warned about a member of staff. I was told he
was difficult. He was a union rep and my fellow managers
distrusted him. However, it was clear that although he had a low
opinion of the company he was very good at his job and cared

greatly about doing a good job. I gradually empowered him and he took on more and more responsibility. I really feel we couldn't do without him because he still has that rigour but it is now harnessed to what we all need to achieve and not his narrow agenda. If I had listened to the grapevine I would have missed a winner.

Method 4: Run a life-story competition or other event
Here, people could write about things they have done, and what they are interested in. This might be a nice way of getting people to open up more about their talents.

One manager ran a getting-to-know you session by offering a balloon ride to his staff. Getting away from the office and creating a fun environment allowed people to get to know each other better and speak more freely about themselves.

Method 5: Set people a specific problem
Use the example of the hotel manager earlier in this chapter. Say to your team 'I think we need to improve X, Y or Z' or 'I'm looking for suggestions about how we might improve A, B or C'. Allow people to come to you with their suggestions and the chances are they are likely to be very motivated.

Winning support

One thing you have on your side with this exercise is that people generally like talking about themselves, so if you give them a chance to talk about what they are interested in, and what they are good at, the chances are that when they feel comfortable and confident to do so, they will. In other words if they don't feel they are going to be persecuted as a result they will be quite open with you.

A cautionary tale

In one organisation a manager asked his people about their interests to find out if he could empower them. One person confessed that he was in, and in fact ran, a new pop band outside work. This entailed many transferable skills. To run a pop band you need to be able to:

- Talk to the press
- Write press releases
- Organise concerts and make sure people, equipment and fans all arrive at the same time
- Keep your chin up when that big break falls through again

Above all, you need to manage a group of diverse and creative people, all of whom want something a little different from the experience and have an opinion to voice. You need to manage their hopes, aspirations and disappointments and keep them focused on the one end: a record deal. Senior management has nothing on making a pop band work! However, the person's manager showed a markedly different response.

Having found out about the pop band, he continued to greet his staff member each day with the embarrassing 'Hello pop star'. It was patently obvious that although desired, pop stardom was still a glimmer on a far horizon. What's more the manager took away all the interesting parts of the staff member's job on the grounds that when pop stardom came, he would inevitably leave at once and so couldn't be trusted with anything interesting.

It is very important that people don't feel threatened by this activity of drawing up a talent rota. Sometimes people may say to you when you ask them about their talents, 'That's none of your business'. Acknowledge they have a right to say this and that they have the right to a private life. However, they will probably only react in this way if they feel they are being quizzed and interrogated about their past and their skills. Try the following four-point plan for overcoming resistance.

Point 1   Make the object of the activity quite clear. Explain that you want to know about their talents in order to help them be more interested and effective at work. It isn't just idle curiosity.

Point 2   You don't want them to feel that you are sucking them dry, or being a leech. So in any of the sessions, it's probably worth telling them about yourself, and the things you enjoy doing, and what you feel you could bring to work but aren't at the moment.

Point 3   The most important thing here is to make this the most supportive part of the empowerment week. Be clear that you aren't looking to turn the information about them against them.

Point 4   It should also be one of the most fun bits because people are being given the chance to talk about and explore the areas they are interested in.

Keep listening
One of the important aspects of this drawing up of a talent rota is that it shouldn't be a one-off event. You need to keep the momentum going so that you are listening, not just over this first week, but over the weeks to come. People may start to feel a bit suspicious if you suddenly come in and start asking questions about what they are interested in, and what they do at the weekend. It needs to be introduced in a more coherent way. They also need to feel that you are going to do something with the information. It's therefore important to stress when you are talking to them that you make it clear that you are looking to use their talents and skills in a project that's coming up, or even in this first empowerment week.

Using the information

The chances are that when you have conducted this exercise you will have a whole mass of paper and ideas that have come in from the people in your team. It's important that you don't let this go to waste, or that you don't lose momentum at this stage.

What you need to do is to start matching up the objectives you have with some of the talents that have been unearthed during the day. You may well be able to use some of these in your 'easy-win' day later in the week.

You might be able to use your talent rota in a number of ways. For instance:

- To match people up with forthcoming events they can contribute towards. If you have unearthed a budding David Bailey have you got an event that needs pictures for the company magazine?
- To identify people who can make an enhanced contribution to the day-to-day work your department does. Have you uncovered a brilliant administrator for instance?
- To develop new areas to capitalise on the skills you unearthed

Are we speaking the same language?

A local authority who carried out this exercise found that they had a remarkable range of people who could speak second languages. The list of languages stretched to over 40 and included Chinese, French, German and a range of languages from Asia. The authority used this finding to develop a new translation service. The reception staff at the town hall were given a directory listing the languages and the people who spoke them. If a person then came into the council and needed a translation service, the people able to offer it were at the end of a telephone.

Summary

Today is an important day because you began exploring what your team really have to offer. This is one of the fundamental ideas behind empowerment. So today you have:

- Examined your attitude to your people and made sure you have the right positive approach
- Looked at some of the hidden talents and life experiences your team have: everyone has something new to give
- Drawn up a talent rota; this will be useful throughout this week and beyond
- Drawn up a first hit list of those people most open to empowerment

Keeping control

So far this week you have:

- Prepared yourself for empowerment
- Examined and planned ways of overcoming some of the barriers to empowerment you face
- Developed some accurate and useful empowerment profiles for your team

It is now time to get down to the business of really making the empowerment happen. Today is about setting some effective empowerment objectives for your team and developing your own empowerment pledge.

One of the main anxieties managers have about empowerment is that they will lose all control and it will become a free-for-all. Indeed, people worry that giving people responsibility is all well and good but in the final analysis, it is your own head that is on the chopping block if the team fails to perform.

Look at the following list of anxieties and see how many you agree with:

> • I fear that my boss will think I am soft if I empower people
> • I will lose all control of my team and they will go off and do what they want
> • People will take liberties the minute I turn back
> • It will be like a runaway train. When people get the idea they can take responsibility how will they know where they are going?
> • It might do me out of a job if people find out my team can get along fine without me. Who needs managers if the staff take all the responsibility?

Clearly effective empowerment shouldn't cause any of these anxieties to become horrible reality. However, you are only human and these kind of thoughts are probably bound to be somewhere in your head. The key thing to realise is that empowerment can be controlled and still thrive.

Plotting a course
Think of it this way. You are setting off from London and you have got to get to Glasgow. Some people may well just set off with a few pounds in their pocket, no map and no timetable, and with no expected time of arrival. These are drifters. Clearly you can't afford to drift. If you were heading to Glasgow you would take with you a route map, an idea of some alternatives, some resources like money and possibly an overnight bag, and you would set yourself a definite time target to reach your destination.

The successful manager of empowerment follows this model and the most important tool of the trade is good, firm empowerment objectives.

The following is a four-step approach to keeping control of your empowerment initiative effectively and negotiating a set of powerful empowerment objectives.

- Step 1: Develop your own empowerment pledge
- Step 2: Do a brief analysis of what people know now
- Step 3: Negotiate
- Step 4: Now write empowerment objectives

Remember, as you work through it, why this is an important exercise.

- If people know where they are going they are likely to feel more enthusiastic about the journey
- Objectives are your way of agreeing what is expected of people
- They are one of the ways you can keep control of empowerment

Step 1: Develop your own empowerment pledge

One problem in setting objectives with people is that it can all seem a somewhat one-way process. Resentment can, and does, build up in a team if they feel they are making all the commitments, doing all the work and taking all the risks. So it's important that you set some objectives for yourself in relation to empowerment and make a clear statement of your own commitments. See this as a sort of empowerment pledge, where you pledge your commitment to empowerment and make a firm statement to your people about what you will do to help them be empowered. They are not looking for an airy statement of intent. They want a firm cast-iron pledge from you.

Write on a sheet of paper *I will*. Then think of five pledges that will be evidence to your own team that you are going to support them to be empowered. For instance you might pledge:

- I guarantee to remove any unnecessary routines by the end of the week

or

- I will make time this week to hold a meeting to canvas ideas on our new initiatives

You will probably come up with a whole load more, but the idea is to develop a pledge to your own people which shows your commitment to empowerment.

You may want to pin up the resultant pledge in the office as a visible symbol, or you may want simply to discuss it with the people in your team so they know you have made a commitment to them and to the empowerment process.

The important thing is that they know you have set your own objectives, and that you are as accountable for the success and failure of empowerment as they are. It is a way of showing that you are not taking the easy route and dumping everything – the responsibility and the work – on to them.

Step 2: Do a brief analysis of what people do now

The first step is to carry out a very brief review of what people do at the moment. It is only when you know what responsibilities and tasks your team do now that you can start setting empowerment activities – which are based on taking on new responsibilities – in the future. For many people the most obvious place to start is the job description. However, beware, because over the years a process of continental drift can take place and job descriptions can bear little resemblance to people's new responsibilities. Instead, ask people to tell you what they do. Get them to write down their main responsibilities and tasks and use this as a first chance to talk through some empowerment possibilities with them. One idea is to ask people to keep a brief work diary outlining what they do. Don't go overboard on this. What you are looking for is just an idea of the main parts of their jobs at the moment. It is important here not to come over as the Gestapo or an old-style work study assessor. Make it very clear that you are *not* checking up on people or trying to spot the workshy ones.

You will probably find that some of your team have already empowered themselves unofficially!

Step 3: Negotiate

Remember, empowerment stresses that people need to be involved in decisions and take responsibility. So if you go away and just draw up a set of objectives which you just present to people and tell them to carry them out you will be undercutting the whole message you are aiming to promote. What you need to do is to involve people in writing their own objectives. This doesn't mean giving them a free hand to decide whatever they want because negotiation is a two-way process. Instead, look at the process of drawing up objectives as a kind of mini version of empowerment itself. And the reason you should aim to negotiate the empowerment objectives? It's simple really. You want people to feel ownership of the whole empowerment process. You want them to take responsibility too. If they feel the objectives are theirs, they are likely to actually attempt to make them a reality.

Here is our action guide to the process of negotiating empowerment objectives with your people.

An action guide to ownership
1 Be clear where you are starting from. You need to get a clear picture of the jobs your people do now in order to negotiate objectives with them for taking on more responsibility. There are a number of techniques you could use, like:

- Getting people to keep job diaries outlining their responsibilities, work patterns and accountabilities

- Asking people to look at their original job descriptions and outlining what new responsibilities they have taken on

When you have done this you need to agree a short analysis of where your team is starting from. It is only when you have a firm idea of the range of responsibilities and tasks your people do now that you can start looking for ways to extend or develop their roles.

2 Be clear before you begin what your organisational objectives are. There is no point setting a perfectly interesting and challenging set of objectives for your people if you need to revisit them again soon after and change them in line with your organisation's priorities. To find out your organisations objectives, look in places like the corporate plan.

It's important to have very clear in your mind what you want to achieve and what your organisation wants to achieve before you sit down and start discussing the objectives for empowerment.

3 Get your people in and talk to them. Because setting objectives is a negotiated process, you need to talk through with your people what they are looking for, and how they think they can make the most contribution to your empowerment goals. There is every possibility that you will agree on what makes a good objective, and in this case everyone can feel

happy. The key word here is ownership. If your
people feel they own their part of the empowerment
process, they are much more likely to go ahead with it,
and flourish within it. Talk through with your people
the purpose of objectives, and your ideas about where
you think the organisation is going. However, don't
crush their ideas. Allow them to have a chance to have
their own input.

4   Always leave yourself enough time to talk through
    objectives with your people. Try to find a quiet place
    where you won't be disturbed by the phone. Give your
    people plenty of time to discuss their hopes and
    aspirations and to make their contribution.

    When you have negotiated some draft objectives give
    your people a chance to go away and reflect and polish
    them. This increases the feeling of ownership still
    further.

5   Meet again and agree the objectives. Sign them off
    formally and keep a record of what you agreed so you
    can come back to it in future.

6   Don't be bullied. You may find that you cannot agree
    the precise details of all the objectives. This is not a
    free-for-all with your people simply demanding what
    they want. You need to make this clear and come with
    objectives that will enable you to reach your team and
    organisational aims. You may need to be firm but fair.
    Above all you will need to be very clear about the
    outcomes you need to deliver.

How do you know whether people feel they own the objectives? Look out for tell-tale signs like:

- People suggesting their own solutions to problems and challenges
- People coming up with a range of new and refined objectives and bringing them to you

If you find people doing either of these then the chances are they feel they own both the process of setting objectives and the objectives themselves.

Step 4: Now write empowerment objectives

There is a neat way of describing how to write effective objectives. It comes as an acronym: SMART, and smart is what you'll be if you stick to the rules laid down here.

Specific

Objectives need to be specific to both the individual and the task to which they relate. They need to be precise so people know exactly what is expected of them. The key thing here is that the people whose objectives they are, need to be able to assess for themselves whether they have actually achieved them. Don't go for general statements like, 'improve customer satisfaction'. These aren't objectives, they are aims. A specific objective might be something like, 'reduce the number of customer complaints received annually'. The thing is that the people who are carrying out the task should be able to check regularly to make sure they are achieving the objective.

Measurable

The big question with an objective is how do you know when you have achieved it? An objective like, 'to understand Total Quality Management' is completely unmeasurable. How do you measure understanding? Much better to say, 'list three key principles of Total Quality Management'. If you can make your objectives easily measurable people will know just what to expect. Again, this is a kind of easy self-check that people can go through when they can see how far they have got towards the empowerment aims they are going for. With empowerment, people need to know where they are going. Because it's new territory, and you are asking them to take responsibility, it would be unfair to tell them simply to go away and come back when they have been empowered, although this kind of thing does happen sometimes.

People need a guide and the most useable and effective guide is a set of firm, solid empowerment objectives.

Empowerment objectives are what allow people to know what is expected of them, where they are going, and how to know when they have got there. It's also your way as a manager of keeping control of the empowerment process, and making sure it is keeping on the right track. Another advantage of objectives is that it allows you to talk to your boss about what you are doing, and show some measurable achievements, later in the week and over the coming months, which will allow the momentum of the empowerment process to carry on.

Achievable

There are two real traps one can fall into with objectives:

- People setting their sights too low (they do this because they are afraid of failing)
- Setting objectives that will never be achieved

You need to come somewhere in the middle. The idea is to produce objectives that are both challenging and achievable. There is nothing more motivating than striving and achieving. However, if people set unattainable objectives the chances are the empowerment process will fizzle out. You need to be realistic about what you expect of your team. For instance, if you are setting up an empowerment process in a restaurant, it would be unrealistic in the first week to expect people to have completely changed their service style. Instead, set objectives that are aware of the real world, and that people are comfortable with.

Relevant

You want to set objectives that are relevant to both the organisation and to the individuals themselves. It's here that you may come into some negotiation with people, because sometimes people's personal goals aren't the same as the goals of the organisation. In an ideal world, of course, the two would be completely compatible, but it's here that you may have some toing and froing to do, and some careful and skilful negotiating to agree them.

Timed
When do you expect people to do what is outlined in the objectives? It may be an obvious point, but is particularly important. Make sure that all of your objectives have a time limit. In the first week it may simply be a set of objectives for the end of the week, which you can measure and see how far you have got. But, remember you will also be setting objectives for the middle and long term as well.

Linking objectives to empowerment
You can use the guidelines above to write any objectives. However, it is important to be absolutely clear that in this case you are writing objectives that are specifically linked

with your empowerment initiative. Make sure there is no confusion about the fact that these are empowerment objectives. The following checklist gives you a way of making the links very clear indeed.

Link them with:

- The aims you set yourself at the start of the week. If your people base their objectives around these you will have a way of measuring your success
- The barriers you identified earlier. You might identify a barrier like the physical environment your team work in. Try to set some objectives for tackling your top barriers
- The ideas for improvement your team have identified so far
- The current job descriptions and responsibilities of your team. You can set specific objectives aimed at stretching people and extending their responsibilities
- Training needs. The chances are that this kind of exercise will expose areas your staff feel weak on. You may be asking people to take more responsibility for financial matters, for instance. In this case you may identify a real training need that could be addressed in an empowerment objective

The important thing here is to make sure you link your empowerment objectives very firmly with service improvement outcomes. You want to link the objectives to real improvements in service standards.

You also need to set review dates so you can revisit the objectives and see how they work out. You may need then to set some revised objectives in order to continue the empowerment process.

Summary

Today you have gone through an important control process. You have looked at the idea behind empowerment objectives and the practical business of writing them. As part of this you have:

- Looked at an important way of controlling the empowerment process
- Looked at the process of setting empowerment objectives. In particular you looked at how to set SMART objectives
- Set some actual empowerment objectives through a negotiated approach. It is negotiation that allows your people to take ownership of the objectives

The 'easy-win' day

Empowerment is new and can be very challenging. People may be sceptical, cynical or simply unsure about the whole process. There may well be people, and sometimes senior people, just waiting to say, 'I told you it wouldn't work'.

It's important, therefore, to score some victories early on. You need to demonstrate that empowerment can and does work, and may well be the way forward for you and your organisation. An 'easy-win' is something you can do at once and which packs a punch.

Clearly, you won't be able to achieve some of your big and long-term aims all at once, but you may in the first few days be able to make a visible difference. The aim is to make people sit up and start to take notice, and realise that things are being done differently, and better too.

There are two important ideas you need to keep in mind as you go about your easy-win day.

Don't underestimate the power of rewards

One of the really good things about this easy-win day is that it gives you the chance to give your people a chance to do some of the things they actually want to do. If someone has been asking for more responsibility, here is your chance to give it to them. If someone has revealed a hidden talent here is your chance to give them a chance to use it. The message is go out and reward your staff.

On an empowerment drive in a hotel, the manager discovered that one of his staff loved doing magic tricks. On his easy-win day he encouraged this staff member to start doing tricks for the children who came into the hotel. This was a powerful reward and motivator for the staff member and made a clear statement to the rest of the staff that empowerment gave them the opportunity to have more interesting and fulfilling jobs.

So, today, is the day when you look to give some rewards. Remember, though, rewards take a variety of shapes and forms.

- What is a reward for one person may seem like a virtual punishment to another
- Some people may be motivated by tangible rewards like being offered a place on a prestigious training course. Others may be switched on by more intangible rewards like a simple 'Well done' from you

On this easy-win day, make sure you match up the right reward with the right person. This is worth emphasising.

One often neglected way of deciding on rewards is actually to ask people what they are looking for. Don't make assumptions about the rewards people are looking for. It is far too easy to dish out rewards that you would like but your people have no interest in.

Thanks, but no thanks

In one organisation a senior manager decided to reward one of her middle managers for some very good performance. She called him into her room and said how well he had done. She then announced that as a reward he would be doing a residential two-week management course. He looked glum because the reward he really wanted was a pay rise, or an extra day's holiday with his family.

One last point here is that praise can be a very powerful reward. However, it is important that your team know that your praise actually means something. This doesn't mean being a praise miser – the kind of boss who need praise wringing out as from a stone. Instead, be clear and praise people when they deserve it and not at the drop of a hat. Your team aren't stupid. Over-praising devalues the whole process.

Another powerful reward is promotion. If your team know that by taking on empowerment and the responsibility that goes with it will help them gain promotion, many of them will quickly buy in.

You may be quite restricted about the rewards you can give, but they are the heart of this easy-win day. Look on it positively. This is your chance to give people what they are looking for.

Gradually turn up the volume
See today as just the start of a much longer process of winning people over. One way of looking at this is that empowerment is something you need to gradually turn up the volume on. In other words, starting today, you aim to encourage people gradually to take on more and more responsibility until they act and feel fully empowered. This may take a number of months but today is where you start.

A manager told us how she went about turning up the volume. Before empowerment she had a member of staff who was demotivated and disruptive but clearly bright and well motivated outside work. On her easy-win day she handed over responsibility for a key part of the department's documentation. The staff member showed an aptitude for this and a few weeks later asked to take control of all department's quality documentation. This process continued and she now is second in command in the department.

So, today is your chance to light those fires of enthusiasm and start thawing any resistance. Why not follow our guide to easy wins for the rest of today?

A guide to easy wins

You can choose any or all of our top tips for empowerment through easy wins. They are in no particular order.

- Learn to like to say 'yes'
- Get and then use a fighting fund
- Identify cast-iron cost-free improvements
- Use positive reinforcement

- Challenge those routines
- Hold a brainstorming session
- Change your style
- Hold your own awards ceremony
- Handover – don't dump

Learn to like to say 'yes'
One of the first things you should do today is show that you can say 'yes' sometimes. One of the things that bedevils any empowerment process is what we call the 'yes, but' syndrome. This means that everyone who comes up with a good idea is confronted with the same answer, 'yes, but. . . and then offered a list of things that say why that idea could never really work in the real world. Today, you need to practice saying 'yes' so people feel motivated and enthusiastic about going away and trying things, within the parameters of the objectives they have set, of course. You might want to do a 'yes, but' count. Every time you or one of your colleagues says 'yes, but' mark it on the flipchart or wall of your office. Promise you will take your people out to lunch if you get above 10 'yes, buts' today. This will act as a tonic for you and will focus your mind on being more positive about the ideas of your people. Alternatively, you could also treat them to lunch if you can keep 'yes, buts' to below five today, just to keep you on your toes.

Get and then use a fighting fund
Money isn't everything and it is perfectly possible to carry out an easy-win day without spending a penny; you might just work on improving your leadership style or carrying out cost-free changes. However, if you can get together a pot

of money that you can use today in order to make a visible difference and show that empowerment works, it can put you at an advantage.

One hospital we worked with managed to get some money for its easy-win day. One of the first suggestions that came up was that patients would like duvets, rather than traditional starchy sheets. There was enough money in the pot to provide duvets for one ward, which were bought on that day. This made a powerful statement that empowerment was happening, that managers were serious about it, and that people's ideas were being listened to.

The key thing, if you have a small fighting fund, is to commit some of it today on a project that will show you are serious about empowerment. You want something that is visible.

As well as using a fighting fund, today may be a chance for you to devolve some budgetary responsibility to your team. Ask yourself whether you can give your people some control over the purse strings. For instance you could:

- Give them discretion to offer small refunds if the service lets a customer down
- Give then a fund they can use to implement ideas for service improvement

Identify cast-iron cost-free improvements
Are there any cost-free improvements you identified earlier in the week that you can now use? We gave the example earlier of the cleaners' uniforms at the hospital that were found in a cupboard, were brought out, dusted down, and became a visible symbol that things were about to change.

Can you think of anything in your organisation that you could do, free of charge, that shows people's ideas are being listened to?

Use positive reinforcement
A good easy win is to make sure you go out and spot something your people are doing *right*. When you witness good empowered behaviour make a note of it and make sure you tell people that they are doing things right.

This means that today you need to make sure you are visible and available. It is no good today shutting the door to your office with a cheery 'go and get on with it'. If you do this, people are likely to shrug their shoulders and do things exactly as they did them last week and the week before and the week before.

Get out and about amongst the troops, and then sit in the background and watch them. Listen to what they are saying. The chances are you will very soon start spotting examples of very good practice. It might simply be someone taking full responsibility for delivering customer service. It may be someone coming up with an idea quickly and putting it into action. Whatever you come across, make sure you praise people. If you can't at the end of the day say you have found two or three things worth praising, then you are not looking properly.

Challenge those routines
Old and unchallenged routines are one of the real enemies of empowerment. They:

- Stifle innovation
- Reinforce old patterns
- Often support bureaucratic ways of doing things

Are there any routines that you could change simply and quickly, to demonstrate that things are about to change?

Hold a brainstorming session
Call a quick 'any ideas' meeting first thing in the morning. Find a quiet room if you can and brainstorm with your people as many ideas for improvement as you can think of to do that day. Don't rule anything out and don't comment negatively or positively on the ideas as you write them down. Try to get everyone to take part but don't force them.

After about 20 minutes take the best five ideas. Analyse them and see which ones:

- You can take on by just walking out of your office and doing something at once
- Your team can do at once

Then go away and make them happen.

Change your style

It doesn't cost anything to change your style and become more participative. However, although this is one of the most obvious avenues and one of the most successful too, managers are often very reluctant to try it. Today, though is the day to take the plunge and dare to be different.

One manager made a change by deciding not to answer every direct request for help with a piece of advice. Instead, she decided to answer questions fired at her by her team with, 'What do you think we should do'? At first this caused a murmur of discontentment because people had become used to relying on her for all the answers and all the guidance, and of course on her taking all the responsibility. However, when they realised that they were going to have to start thinking for themselves and actually had the power to go away and do things, this quickly unlocked a whole

bunch of ideas and accessed some of their hidden potential.
You might use the following answers during today to help
you get people thinking about what they could do
differently. This is another kind of easy win.

Some answers
- I'm not sure about the answer to that. What do you think we should do?
- Go and write down some ideas, and come back to me with what you think the answer might be
- I'm a bit stuck. Can you think of a way we might get around this problem?
- I've tried a few ideas but I think we could probably come up with some better ones. What do you think?
- I've cleared it with my boss. I'd like you to go and sit on the steering group meeting, and come back with some ideas we might use in this department

Some people have analysed the above approach and come
up with the name *'transactional analysis'*. This is based on the
simple idea that all of us take up certain roles when we
interact with people. The most obvious are the parent-child
roles. In other words in any relationship one person takes on
the role of parent and offers advice and takes control and
responsibility. The other person takes on a child role which
is passive. Obviously, we take on different roles with
different people. With some we may be a child and others
we take on the parent role. However, the message is
obvious. In many organisations, staff take on a childlike
role. They are dependent on their boss and are fearful of
taking responsibility. They are often fearful because their
organisation punishes any mistake they make when they

take the initiative. The boss becomes a kind of workplace parent, soaking up the pressure and giving all the advice. For empowerment to work you need to break this cycle. A powerful way to do this is to change your style.

With empowerment you are aiming, through your style and actions, to shift your people away from the child role and into the parent role; taking full responsibility for their actions. You won't do this at once, but you will need to reinforce the message continually that you won't take all of their worries on to your shoulders and that they must take responsibility for their own work. You need to work at letting go and get your people used to standing on their own two feet.

Hold your own awards ceremony
At the end of today, find 15 minutes to hold an impromptu and fun awards ceremony for your team. Surprise them with it before everyone goes home. Explain to them that you have been impressed with all their hard work and the glee with which they decided to do you out of a job. Present a daft award for the best bit of empowerment, the most empowered person of the day and maybe give a spoof award for the least successful too.

Have fun and use this as a way of developing the team feeling and commitment to empowerment.

Handover – don't dump
Remember empowerment is not about dumping all the jobs you don't fancy on to your people and keeping all the good stuff for yourself. It has to be meaningful to them; not just giving them a choice of whether to buy the office envelopes

from WH Smiths or Rymans. *Don't* follow the following guide:

> *A devil's guide to empowerment*
> - I hate that job, I don't mind handing it over
> - There's no money to do that job properly, let them struggle with it
> - It's his fault it went wrong, I delegated it to him
> - Don't disturb me for the next two weeks, I've got a job to do on my computer
> - I can't give you the reason for my decision. Just do it, and sharp
> - I want all the interesting work
> - I want all the work that gets the praise, you can have the low status stuff
> - I'm really glad you've done all that hard extra work. Now my boss will think *I'm* wonderful

As you develop ideas for your easy-win day, keep 'what not to do' guide in mind. You may even decide to hand over a job you particularly enjoy and your team know you particularly enjoy.

Team formation

A little word of warning. If you find getting easy wins hard going don't lose heart. Remember, you are trying to make a major change in the way people think and behave at work. You may notice disruptive behaviour, but don't throw in the towel and run back to the comfort of the way things used to be. One way of understanding that easy wins – and indeed any progress to start with – may be difficult is to think about the way teams form and respond to change. The following is one model.

Forming
The team comes together
Storming
The team starts testing the limits of the leader's authority and their own roles. People's behaviour may be disruptive
Norming
The team starts to accept the new way of doing things and their own changed roles
Performing
Bingo! The team work effectively under the new regime
Mourning
Sometimes the team feel a sense of anticlimax

When you introduce or make empowerment happen you need to move your team through these phases. So, in this first week, stay calm if it seems difficult to move your team beyond 'storming'.

Summary

Today, we have looked at the whole idea of easy wins.
These are important because they show that things will be
different and that empowerment really can work, both for
staff and in terms of delivering better service. We looked at:

- Why it is so important to provide easy wins for
  empowerment initiatives
- How to go about putting together an easy-win day
  for your team

The importance of good communication

It has been said that without information you cannot be empowered and that with information you cannot but be empowered. These are wise words.

Communication is the real life blood of empowerment. You need to make sure your communications are working in a number of different ways. People need to know:

- What's expected of them. Empowerment can be confusing and can sweep away the old certainties. The message is that your people shouldn't come running to you whenever they have a problem or need a decision about something. Because of this they may experience periods of anxiety. They need to know what you expect from them and whether they are 'doing it right'. We looked at this in the objectives section.

- How they can communicate their ideas for improvement. One of the pay-offs of empowerment is that you should start to generate ideas for service improvement from individuals on the front line, those who know the job and its demands the best. Because you don't want these ideas getting lost in the system or failing to be turned into action, you need to make sure your door is always open and that you regularly get out to talk to people about their work, ideas, aspirations and anxieties.

  If people feel their ideas are not being taken into consideration they will soon switch off and decide that empowerment is simply a fad.

- How the team can come up with ideas for improvement. Sometimes ideas will be generated by the team as a whole. You need to establish some kind of forum whereby the team can explore new ideas and approaches and then use this to start changing the way they work together. This is an important way you can start the process of your team taking responsibility. Every time they come up with an improvement idea it shows they have taken ownership of the service you are providing. They are personally involved.

- How you are going to publicise your successes. Part of the empowerment process is celebrating your successes. You need to communicate to your boss, his or her boss and your team's colleagues in the organisation what you are doing, why you are doing it and how well it is working.

- How you will keep in touch with what your organisation expects. The chances are you are working on empowerment as part of an organisation- or division-wide initiative. You need to be absolutely clear about what is expected of you and your team. Obviously, your organisation will have communication channels, be they appraisal meetings with your boss, magazines or briefings. However you need to be pro-active and make sure you keep up with your organisation's current thinking on empowerment. Make sure you know what is expected.

So you are sharpening communications in four main directions and in each area you need to review your communication systems.

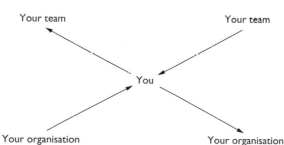

An empowerment communications model

The key to looking at communication is to be broad in your approach. You need a range of different methods to make sure the empowerment message is kept alive, and that people are constantly clear about what it is you are trying to achieve. Here are just some suggestions.

You to them

You will have to become an unofficial salesperson. You need to be constantly selling the idea of empowerment to your people. It is likely as time goes on that you will need to do this less and less. But, at least for the first few weeks you will need to be constantly outlining benefits, highlighting examples and stating why you are going to all the time and trouble.

Don't worry if you sound a bit like a record with the needle stuck.

Objectives

We looked in detail earlier in the week at objectives. These still remain one of the main ways of communication between you and your people. Refresh your memory today about the ones you all set, including the ones you have set for yourself.

Interpersonal communication

You need to make time to talk to your people. Probably the best way to do this today is simply to be available, and to walk around your department, finding time to discuss what they are doing, and if they are finding any difficulties with the empowerment process. If you do this exercise, be prepared for some surprises. People may comment on your own performance. If you ask people if they are having difficulties they will probably tell you about them, so you need to find time to listen to them properly and then to act on your findings.

There is a simple cycle at work here.

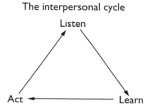

The interpersonal cycle

In many ways you need to learn afresh how to listen to your people and then act. Part of this might be simply looking for small verbal clues which show uncertainty or unease. Remember, communication is an active process. It is also linked to an end result. There is no point simply soaking up all your team's suggestions like a sponge and then doing nothing with them.

Your job is to reinforce the empowerment message and to help people continually focus on what's expected of them. Your job is also to continue the process of giving positive reinforcement. This is probably one of your biggest weapons. People are used to being told they have done things wrong, and it can come as quite a shock to be told they have done things right.

Briefing notes
Because empowerment seems quite intangible, people can seem to keep losing the thread. Don't become impatient with this. People may be changing the habits of a working lifetime when they start to take full responsibility.

What you need to do is keep people up to date with how you are thinking and what you expect of them. So, today might be the day to put together a short briefing note explaining and reinforcing why you are going for empowerment, what you want from it and what you have done already. This acts as a good reminder for members of your team and gives them confidence that you know where you are going.

Rallying calls
At the start of today why not call your team together just for five minutes. Then:

- Congratulate them on what they have achieved so far during the week
- Explain to them what you have done yourself: any meetings you have had with other people in the organisation or anything you have done to push empowerment along
- Pick out any particular examples of good practice that have emerged so far
- Reiterate any goals you as a team have set yourselves
- Encourage your team to carry on the good work and stress that if they need to talk, you are available. At least in the first few weeks, as people get used to the idea and reality of empowerment, you will need to be very available and expect much of your time to be taken up with simply talking and listening to people

Them to you

So far you have looked at how to improve communication for empowerment from you to your team. But what about from them to you?

The main focus here is that you need to make sure the individuals in your team and your team as a whole can communicate all their ideas for improvement as they happen and that they feel confident that something will happen as a result.

There are many ways of going about this and the following offers just one very brief snapshot.

Empowerment circles

One of the ideas behind empowerment is that people on the front line probably have much better ideas for improving service than their managers, if only they were given the chance to express them. You need to get these ideas out in to the open regularly.

One way is to set up an empowerment group where people get together informally and discuss ways of making the organisation more empowered, more customer focused and more effective. This is how to set up and run one.

- Ask all your team to attend. Explain that everyone has a vital part to play and all views will be listened to
- Explain the purpose of the empowerment circle informally to those who are taking part. Namely: to explore ideas and suggestions for making empowerment work and to give better customer service as a result
- Set aside a time and place for the meeting, probably about an hour, and in a quiet room if possible
- Meet
- Hand the chairing of this group over to one of your team to make a visible sign that you aren't directing everything. You might want to be the person with the pen, standing by the flipchart ready to write down the ideas that come up. You don't want an agenda; instead you are just looking for ideas and ways forward
- At the end of each session come up with a list of the ideas for improvement that have been suggested, and then some ways forward

You to the organisation

This is important and it is an area that many managers leave out because it seems difficult. However, you do need continually to make sure you get your team's achievements with empowerment out into your organisation. Remember, people won't know what you are doing or what you have done unless you show them *and* tell them.

In many organisations, this means you need to behave politically, always looking to score a win for your team and for empowerment as well.

Many managers are very uncomfortable with this political aspect but there really isn't any need to be. Many people have the cripplingly naïve belief that if you turn up to work, be a good person and do your best then you will be recognised. This is patently untrue. You need to work at your PR in work. This is particularly important if you are embarking on a new initiative like empowerment. You need always to look for opportunities to discuss your team's work, *and* to spread the word. You need to identify the people who can help or hinder you and work on them. Remember your own personal standing is at stake. So go out there and enjoy being political with a small 'p'.

Celebrate your successes   If one of your team, or your team as a whole, comes up with a good idea or shows good practice then celebrate the success. You might hold a small celebration or just take an opportunity to tell people what happened. You might ask people to meet after work when something good happens. You might be able to feed a story to your company press office, if you have one. Invite your boss along or maybe other front-line people in the organisation to any event. Hand out gold stars or award an empowered employee a prize. Remember if you succeed, tell people. People who hear will act as ambassadors for empowerment and may well spread the message into new areas in the organisation.

Work on your allies Earlier in the week you identified your allies outside the department who you felt might support you. Give them a ring or make sure you bump into them. Give them a brief, realistic but upbeat appraisal of what your team have been doing. Talk to more senior people about your team's work and watch the pond start to ripple.

Work on your enemies We will look in more detail at this tomorrow. It is important, though, to review again who is standing in your way and refusing to buy in.

The organisation to you

This is quite straightforward. Keep in touch with what your organisation expects. Find out if there are any new ideas buzzing around. Are there any new directives from senior managers you should follow? Keep your ear to the ground. Do a scanning exercise. Are there any documents or important meetings you should attend? Have there been any subtle shifts of emphasis?

Summary

Today, we worked on improving communications for empowerment. Communications are at the heart of empowerment and need to be constantly reviewed and sharpened.

We looked at:

- How to improve the way you communicate with your people; there are a number of methods here
- Opening a vital channel for them to communicate their ideas with you through an empowerment circle or non-agenda meeting
- Spreading the message of empowerment and your team's role wider in the organisation
- Monitoring the situation from the organisation itself to make sure you are still on the right lines

Review

Well, you've got through the week and it's now time to take stock. The chances are you found it demanding. Some things probably didn't go according to plan.

You need to ask yourself.

- What have I learned and achieved?
- Where am I going in the future?

What have I learned?

Find somewhere quiet where you can think. Get together any notes or ideas you jotted down during the week.

You need to get your mental approach right; try to be honest and don't be too impatient or hard on yourself. Getting empowerment working takes time and effort. This week, you were really laying the foundations for your work in the future.

Now, write down all the things that have gone well, and all the mistakes you think you have made, or things you think you could have done better. Remember the idea is to see what you can learn from the experience of last week.

You might want to use the following as headings:

- The people who bought in and made a real contribution and those who did not
- The processes that worked and those that could still be improved over the coming week
- The barriers that remain to be broken down and those we have overcome this week

The idea at the end is to come up with a list of five or six things you think you have learned during the week. Remember though, empowerment isn't something you can hurry.

What you may have done this week is to start lighting fires of enthusiasm and picking up some converts along the way. You have probably also developed some examples of good practice that you can bring up in your team briefing first thing next Monday. And remember, try to keep as upbeat as you can, but be realistic.

Test it out
One way of testing your progress is to run through some scenarios in your head and think how they would have been tackled before you started empowerment and now at the end of this first week. Here are some suggestions.

- A customer has a complaint about the service he or she received. How will they be dealt with by your team member? Will you need to get involved? Can your person give a refund?

- A team member has an idea for improving customer service. It is quick and cheap to initiate. How easy would it have been to get this idea into practice last week and at the end of this week? Would it have to go to committee or through you for approval?

- A customer has managed to lose his ticket (or receipt or whatever). Has your front-line person got the power to sort the problem out?

Where am I going?

Empowerment is more of a marathon than a 100 metres sprint, so start setting yourself long-term goals for the coming weeks and months.

Looking back at the achievements and learning opportunities you identified, what goals will you set for yourself in the next:

- Week?
- Month?
- Six months?

Ask yourself if you will need any extra resources and help.

Develop a plan
Having decided on some objectives, you now need to put together a simple action plan. You can base it around a set of simple questions.

- What do we want to achieve? These are the objectives you set yourself
- How are we going to achieve it? You need to be clear about what you and your team will do to make your plan a success
- Who will achieve it? Who are your key players and what jobs are they going to carry out?
- When will we achieve it by? What are your timescales and landmark dates?
- How will we know we achieved it? How will we monitor and measure our success?

You need to set targets in the short, medium and long term.

Summary

Today we took stock and made plans for the future. In particular we:

- Looked at what you have learned during the week
- Looked at what barriers still exist
- Tested out some empowerment scenarios to see what has changed during the week
- Developed objectives and an action plan for the future

Remember, empowerment is an on-going process. Feel free to revisit this book over the next few weeks so you can try out new ideas and explore areas you didn't touch first time around.